Meet the Boys!

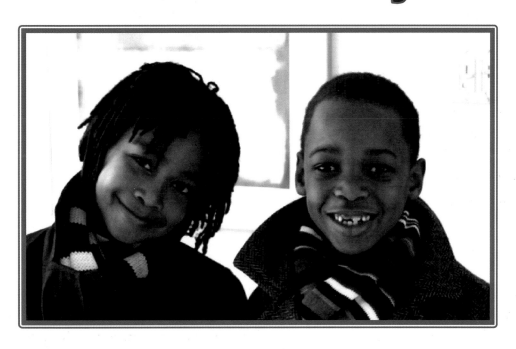

By MaryAnn McAlpin
Photos by James Napoli

I am Luca.

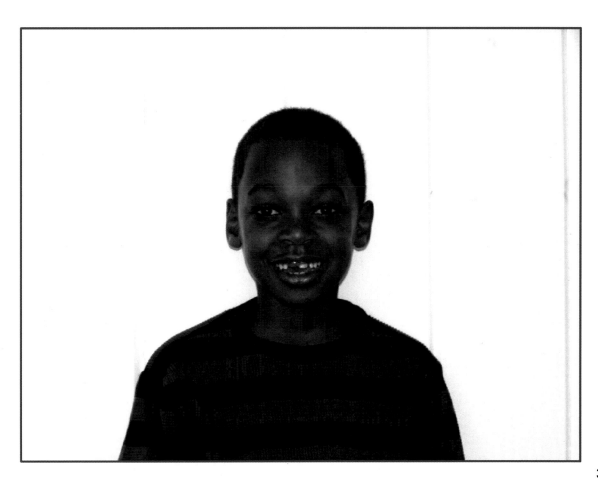

3

I am Anthony.

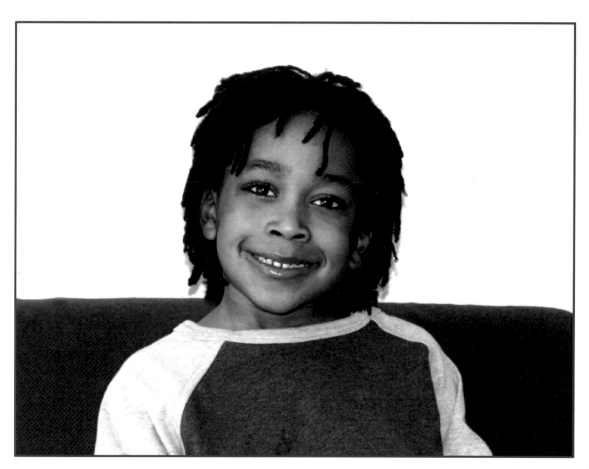

We are brothers.

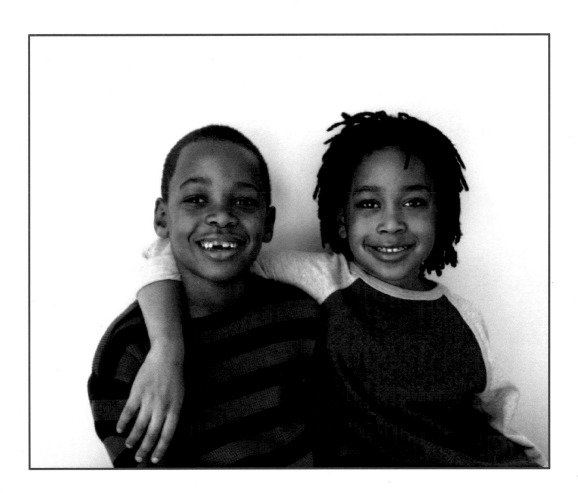

We like to play together.

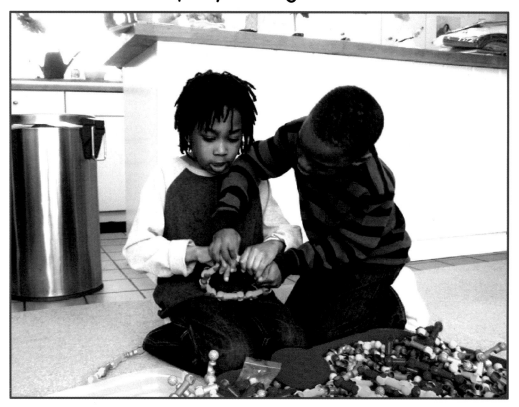

We like to eat together.

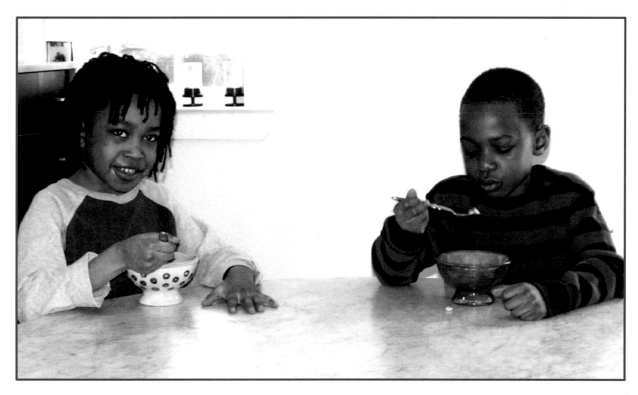

We like to read together.

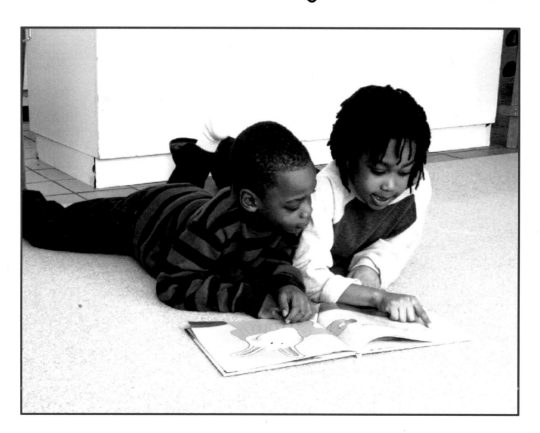

We like to work together.

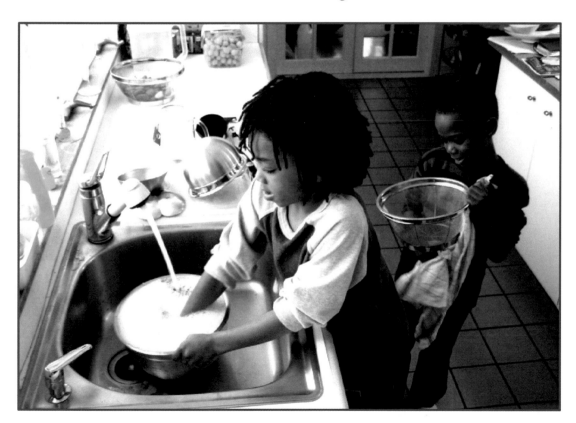

We are brothers!
We like to be together!

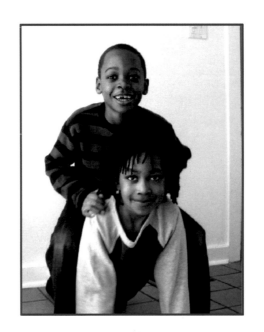